DIAMOND ENGAGEMENT RING

BUYING GUIDE

9 Secret Questions that your Jeweller doesn't want you to know

DIAMOND ENGAGEMENT RING

BUYING GUIDE

9 Secret Questions that your Jeweller doesn't want you to know

Puneet Mehra

Available on amazonkindle

Worldwide Published by

Pendown Press

PREMIUM BUSINESS PUBLISHER

PENDOWN PRESS LLP
An ISO 9001 & ISO 14001 Certified Co.,
Regd. Office: 3767A, Kanhaiya Nagar,
Tri Nagar, Delhi-110035
Ph.: 8130886000, 9650072927
E-mail: info@pendownpress.com
Branch Office: 1A/2A, 20, Hari Sadan, Ansari Road,
Daryaganj, New Delhi-110002
Ph.: 011-45794768
Website: PendownPress.com

Edition: 2025
Price: ₹ 399
ISBN: 978-93-7217-342-0

Layout and Cover Designed by Pendown Graphics Team
Printed and Bound in India by Thomson Press India Ltd.

Dedicated to all those who believe a ring is more than jewellery; it's love, commitment, and a promise in one small circle.

TABLE OF CONTENTS

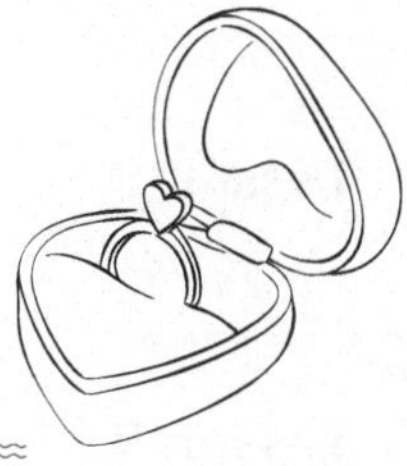

PREFACE

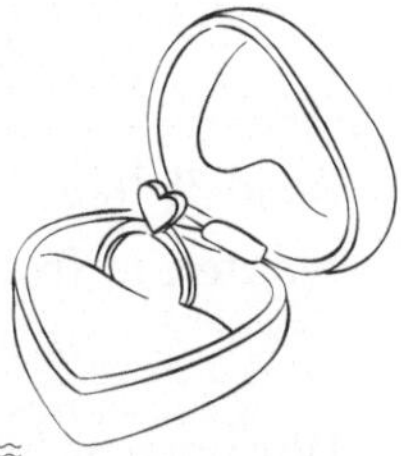

This book was born out of one simple thought: *Why is buying a diamond so confusing?*

Over the years, I've watched many people walk into showrooms with big dreams and walk out with even bigger doubts. Some didn't know what questions to ask. Some trusted the wrong advice. And many just nodded along, pretending to understand terms they had never even heard before.

I've been in this field long enough to know one thing: *diamonds may be rare, but honest information about them is even rarer.*

This book isn't written to sell you anything. It's written to guide you. To make you feel confident instead of confused. To help you understand what really matters when buying a diamond, not just the shine, but the story behind it. Not just the beauty you see, but the value you deserve.

Whether you're buying your first ring, replacing an old one, or simply curious about how it all works, this book is for you. You don't need to know anything about diamonds before opening these pages. You don't even need to be a reader, just a learner with good intentions.

I've kept the language simple. I've kept the chapters short and easy. I've shared what I've seen, what I've learned, and what I wish every buyer knew before making this meaningful purchase.

Read it like a friend is talking to you. Because that's how I've written it, from one heart to another.

With warmth,

Puneet Mehra

Acknowledgements

Whatever I have achieved in life, would have been impossible without the support of my parents. They've taught me unconditional love and I have seen them grow along with me. The wings that I have today would not have been possible without them.

To my wife, Nidhi, who has stood by me in every situation. You have handled all family responsibilities with great skill and dedication. Thank you from the bottom of my heart.

To my children, Lavanya and Naman, who are the source of my happiness and inspiration. Lots of love!

My heartfelt gratitude to all my mentors and guides who have shown me light and direction in times of confusion.

To our clients, who have shared their experiences and knowledge with us during this journey, thank you for trusting us and being our inspiration.

To my team, your commitment, creativity and constant support have played a huge role in making this dream come true. You are the backbone of everything we do, and I feel proud to have you by my side.

A special acknowledgement goes to Dinesh Verma and his exceptional team at Pendown Press. From the initial concept to the final manuscript, their support and expertise have made this book possible.

And finally, to all my loved ones who have been with me on this journey, thank you for your unwavering support, encouragement, and affection. Even if your names are not mentioned, you always hold a special place in my heart.

Without the support of all of you, it would not have been possible for me to move forward with confidence.

AUTHOR'S CORNER

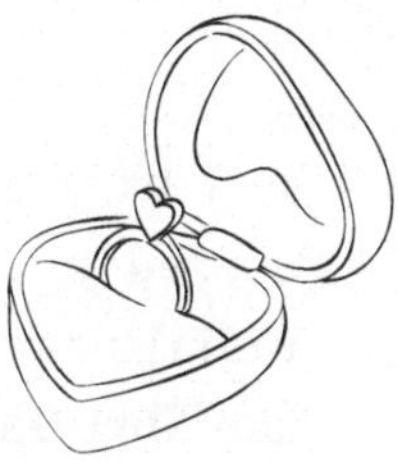

Hello, my name is Puneet Mehra. I am a **fourth-generation jeweller** and a certified gemmologist, having graduated from the **Geological Institute of America (GIA)**. I also hold the distinction of being a **government-approved jewellery valuer**, appointed by the **Ministry of Finance, Government of India**, a recognition that underscores my credibility and expertise in this field. With over 30 years of hands-on experience in jewellery manufacturing, design, and retail, I proudly carry forward the legacy of a family deeply rooted in the world of fine jewellery for **four generations**. Our heritage is not just a story; it's a responsibility that I embrace every day with passion and purpose.

For three generations, our family exclusively served the **business-to-business (B2B)** segment. It was only in **1991**, when my brother **Vanit Mehra** took a bold step to open our **first retail store in Lajpat Nagar**, that we began reaching out to individual customers. I joined him in **1996**, marking the start of a new chapter, one that combined our rich legacy with a modern retail approach.

As a child, I always dreamt of becoming an airplane pilot. I was fascinated by how planes fly and longed to travel the world. To my younger self, being a pilot seemed like the perfect and easy way to travel the world. But life, as it often does, had other plans and they turned out to be more fulfilling than I ever imagined.

My great-grandfather, grandfather, and father were all jewellers, so I truly have jewellery in my blood. My great-grandfather opened a jewellery store in 1932 in **Lahore (pre-partition India)**, naming it **Gandaram Jewellers** after my grandfather, the late **Shri Gandaram Mehra**. In 1947, my grandfather opened a store in **Chandni Chowk** in partnership with **Mr. Ramgopal**, named **GandaRam Ram Gopal Jewellers**, and then in 1955, he opened a store in Dariba Kalan, Delhi. Over the years, I have successfully continued our family legacy, running the jewellery store for over 30 years in Lajpat Nagar, New Delhi, along with my father, Mr. Vipin Mehra.

Our journey has been incredible. What sets us apart is our **commitment to authenticity and control over our creations**. We are not traders, we are makers. Every piece of jewellery is born from scratch in our workshop. From **designing diamond rings**, **sourcing and cutting rough diamonds**, to **crafting the final product**, we oversee every detail. This gives us not only **confidence** in what we sell but also the **ability to stand behind each piece with full integrity**, knowing exactly what it's made of and how it's made.

WHY THIS BOOK?

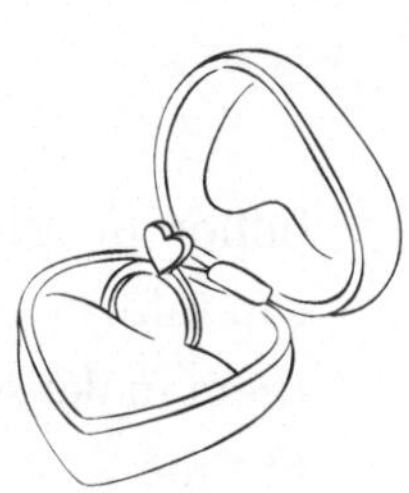

You might be wondering why I am writing this book. There are two main reasons: First, I have a deep love for diamonds. Second, over the years, I've observed a curious trend. Brides and grooms spend hours selecting their bridal outfits, often spending a fortune on dresses from top designers, which they will wear only for four to six hours on their wedding day. Yet, when it comes to something as significant as a diamond engagement ring, something they'll wear every single day for the next 80 years or more, they often visit just any local jeweller and make a rushed decision.

I believe a diamond engagement ring should bring joy every single time it's worn, because it's not just jewellery, **it's a symbol of your love story**, one that stays with you for life. Every glance at it should spark happiness, and every compliment it receives should make the wearer feel proud to say, *'It's from Gandaram Jewellers.'* We want our customers to feel that deep emotional connection, that pride in the quality, beauty, and meaning behind their ring.

In today's market, the diamond and gold industry is riddled with malpractice, ranging from jewellers selling low-quality materials to cutting corners just to make hidden profits. With intense competition, many prioritize margins over integrity, leaving customers unaware, misinformed, and often disappointed later. As an individual jeweller, I can't personally educate every single person, especially in a vast country like India with over 1.4

billion people. But a book has the power to reach the masses. It can inform, empower, and protect countless individuals, helping them make smarter, more confident decisions in a short amount of time.

That's why I've chosen to write this book**: to share my knowledge, expose the truth, and guide people in making the right decisions** when it comes to buying gold and diamonds. This isn't just a book; it's a tool to help you navigate an industry that often doesn't reveal everything you need to know.

You've found the love of your life, and now it's time to find the perfect symbol of that love, because, as we know, diamonds are a girl's best friend. Her engagement ring is one of the most significant purchases you'll ever make. She will wear it every day for the rest of your lives, and it will quietly yet powerfully symbolize the beautiful, meaningful love you share.

Are you feeling the pressure to find the perfect engagement ring? That's exactly why I am writing this book. The truth is: **the key to finding the right ring is knowing the right questions to ask your jeweller.** By asking the right questions, you'll filter out uncertainty and narrow your options until that one perfect diamond ring reveals itself, shining as brightly as your intentions behind it.

There is no greater satisfaction for me than when someone wears a diamond ring we've created, receives heartfelt compliments, and then takes the time to personally call me or leave a kind google review online. Those moments are deeply fulfilling, they remind me **why I do what I do.** Knowing I've played a part in someone's happiness, especially during such a meaningful occasion, is what keeps me alive with purpose. It fuels my passion and drives me to keep pushing the boundaries of creativity, craftsmanship, and innovation, especially in bridal jewellery design.

I hope the expertise I've gained over my life, which I'm sharing in this book, will help you select the perfect diamond engagement ring. May you enjoy wearing it proudly for the rest of your life, showing it off to your family and friends, not just for how it looks, but for what it represents.

For Whom Is This Book?

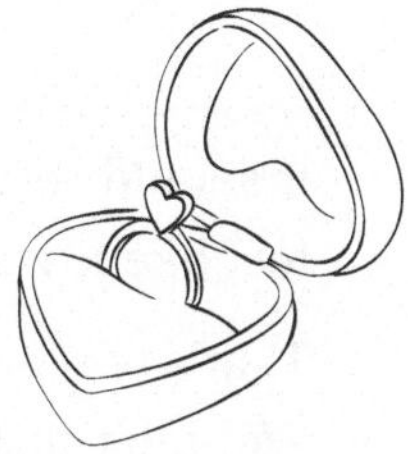

Every man and woman desires to feel appreciated when they wear their diamond engagement ring. It's not just about the sparkle; it's about the **respect, recognition, and emotional connection** that come with it. A well-crafted ring allows them to flaunt it confidently, wear it comfortably, and feel proud every time someone notices it.

But this connection goes deeper, it's about the soul. It's about knowing they've invested their hard-earned money into something **real, honest, and valuable.** In a world full of glittering distractions and misleading deals, **authenticity matters more than ever**. For those who seek truth and craftsmanship, and refuse to be misled or shortchanged, a truly meaningful diamond ring becomes more than jewellery. It becomes a **symbol of love, commitment, and trust**.

Let me share a story that's very close to my heart. One of my very satisfied customers once introduced me to a client who was the head of a large joint family. Traditionally, his family had always purchased jewellery from their long-standing family jeweller, someone they had trusted for generations. However, when it came time to buy an engagement ring for his daughter, he agreed to meet me perhaps out of curiosity, or maybe because of the trust his friend placed in me.

During our meeting, I shared my belief: **selling jewellery isn't just about taking something out of the showcase and closing a deal.** A diamond ring should **reflect the wearer's personality**, it should resonate with their style, spirit, and identity. It should feel like *it was always meant to be theirs.*

That's why we don't follow the typical 'show-and-sell' approach. We don't just open boxes and display rings randomly. Instead, we offer a carefully curated, customized experience. Our highly trained staff first observes the client's body structure, skin tone, hand shape, and even the length and curvature of their fingers. Only then do we suggest the ideal ring design and the most flattering metal color, gold, rose, platinum for their diamond engagement ring.

This thoughtful, personalized approach sets us apart because for us, it's not just about selling a piece of jewellery. It's about crafting a symbol of love and elegance that truly belongs to the person wearing it.

That conversation left an impression. I proudly told him, "If you search on Google for the top three jewellery stores in Delhi, our name appears among them, ranked third." I invited him to read our reviews. He did, right then and there.

He was genuinely impressed by what he read: real stories from real people who appreciated our quality, honesty, and personalized service. That moment changed everything.

Not only did he choose us for his daughter's diamond engagement ring, but he also entrusted us with the complete wedding jewellery.

Today, I'm proud to say that he has become one of our strongest advocates, referring many new clients to us over the years. Every referral is not just business; it's a reflection of the **trust, satisfaction, and relationships** we aim to build with each customer.

This book is for **people like him. And people like you.**

It's for anyone who wants more than just a diamond, who wants a ring that speaks, lasts, and truly belongs.

So, without further ado, let's explore the **Nine Secret Lessons Your Jeweller Doesn't Want You to Know.**

LESSON 1

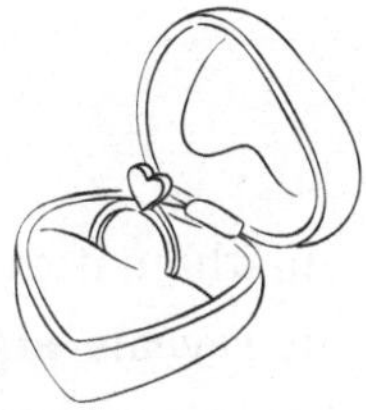

The Secret Geometry

Why Hearts & Arrows Round Brilliant Cut Diamonds Truly Dazzle (and Why Your Jeweller Might Not Push Them)

Diamond Cut: Why You Should Always Choose a Hearts and Arrows Cut for Brilliant Round Diamonds?

The Sparkle That Spoke Louder Than Words

A few years ago, a young man named Rohan walked into my showroom, visibly nervous. He was preparing to propose to his long-time girlfriend, Meera, someone he described as "simple, elegant, and full of grace." He said he wanted a ring that would mirror who she was, something timeless and extraordinary.

I showed him a range of high-quality round brilliant diamonds, but I noticed he kept hesitating. "These are beautiful," he said, "but I want something... more meaningful. Something that will take her breath away."

That's when I introduced him to the **Hearts and Arrows cut**.

I explained to him that this isn't just any round diamond. It's a super ideal cut, where every single facet is aligned with mathematical precision. When viewed under a special scope, it reveals **eight perfect hearts from the bottom and eight precise arrows from the top**. This visual perfection is a result of elite craftsmanship, something only about **10 out of every 100 round diamonds** ever achieve.

This cut doesn't just sparkle," I told him. "It dances with light. It sings when it catches the eye. And more than anything, it reflects the care, effort, and attention to detail you're putting into this moment.

Rohan was intrigued. I handed him the viewing scope so he could see the pattern himself. The moment he saw the perfectly formed arrows glinting in symmetry, he paused. "It's flawless," he said softly. "Just like her."

He bought the ring, a platinum band holding a 1.20 carat Hearts and Arrows diamond.

A few weeks later, he called me.

She said yes," he told me, his voice filled with joy. But do you know what stunned her the most? The way **the diamond sparkled under the sunset**. She kept staring at it and said, 'It looks like it was made for me.'

Today, that couple still refers new clients to us. But what stayed with me the most was Meera's feedback when she visited the store later:

It doesn't just feel like a diamond. It feels like love, frozen in time.

Why Cut Is the Soul of a Diamond

That's the magic of a Hearts and Arrows cut. It's not just about symmetry or light reflection. It's about **precision. Emotion.**

Symbolism. And when done right, it becomes more than jewellery; it becomes a story that lasts forever.

When buying a solitaire diamond, most people focus primarily on color and clarity, often overlooking one of the most important aspects: **the cut.** A diamond without a proper cut is just a dull stone. The brilliance, fire, and sparkle of a diamond all depend on how well it is cut, making it the most crucial factor in determining a diamond's beauty.

However, many jewellers fail to educate their customers about the importance of cut quality. Why? Because it's easier to sell diamonds based on color and clarity alone. These are simpler to explain, and often allow for better profit margins.

In India, **99% of customers are unaware of the "Hearts and Arrows" cut,** simply because most jewellers do not inform them about it. Instead, these premium-cut diamonds are often exported to the U.S. and European markets, where buyers are more informed and willing to pay a premium for superior brilliance.

Why Cut Quality Matters More Than Size or Clarity

In today's diamond market, **cut quality is often compromised in favor of carat weight**. Rough diamond manufacturers, driven by profit margins, shape diamonds to retain more weight, even if it means compromising proportions. The result? A bigger diamond, yes, but one that **fails to shine**.

This is why many jewellers in India sell so-called "Good" or "Very Good" cut diamonds at heavy discounts. It looks like a good deal but in reality, you're buying a diamond that won't sparkle the way it should. That "deal" comes at the cost of brilliance and ultimately, beauty.

What is a Hearts and Arrows Cut?

A Hearts and Arrows cut is the most precisely cut round brilliant diamond. When viewed under a 10X magnification loupe, you will see:

- Arrows when looking at the diamond from the top (table view).
- Hearts when looking at the diamond from the bottom (pavilion view).

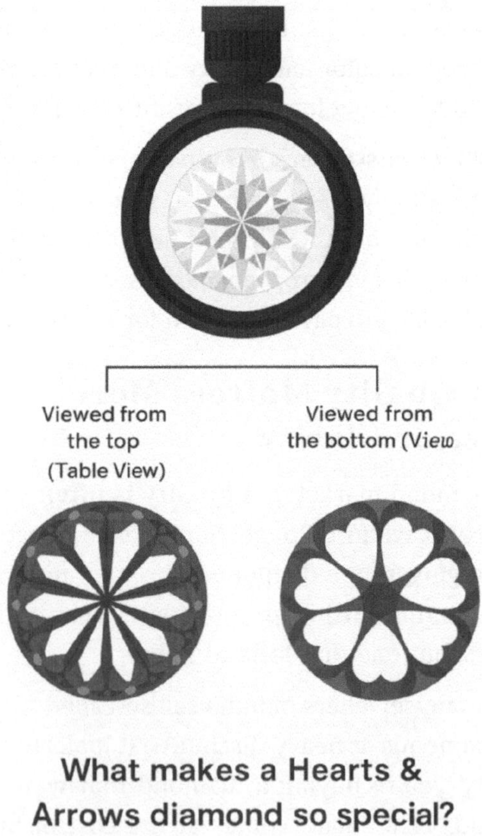

This pattern is a result of perfect symmetry and optimal proportions, ensuring maximum light reflection and brilliance. Only the finest craftsmanship can achieve this precision, making it one of the most sought-after cuts in the world.

Why You Should Always Choose a Hearts and Arrows Cut

1. **Unmatched Brilliance**: The precision of this cut allows the diamond to reflect light in the most efficient way, resulting in a stunning sparkle.
2. **Superior Light Performance**: A poorly cut diamond leaks light, making it appear dull, even if it has high color and clarity. A Hearts and Arrows diamond, however, reflects almost all incoming light, maximizing brilliance.
3. **Higher Perceived Size**: Thanks to their exceptional brilliance, they appear larger than a poorly cut diamond of the same weight.
4. **Better Investment**: These diamonds retain their value better because of their rarity, superior craftsmanship, and international demand.

How to Identify a Well-Cut Diamond

- **For Round Brilliant Diamonds:** Always ask for a Hearts and Arrows cut and verify with a scope or viewer.
- **For Fancy Shapes (Oval, Princess, Emerald, etc.):** Look for diamonds with Excellent Cut, Excellent Polish, and Excellent Symmetry to achieve the best sparkle.

Final Advice: Don't Settle for Less

Most jewellers in India will try to sell you a "Good" or "Very Good" cut diamond at a discounted price while making hidden profits.

Don't fall for this trap. Instead, ask specifically for a Hearts and Arrows cut when buying a round brilliant cut solitaire, and go for Excellent Cut, Polish, and Symmetry in fancy shapes.

Your diamond is a once-in-a-lifetime investment, make sure it shines at its absolute best.

LESSON 2

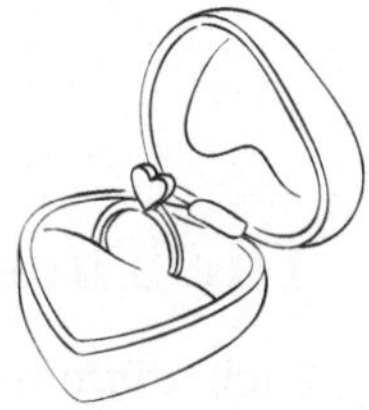

Seeing Clearly
A Jeweller's Tale About Diamond Clarity

IS THE DIAMOND EYE-CLEAN OR JUST PAPER-CLEAN?

Clarity. To most people, it's just a technical term on a grading chart. But to me, after decades of working with diamonds, clarity is something much deeper. It's a quiet story that each stone whispers... if you know how to listen.

The Day Maya Returned

It was a calm afternoon when I saw Maya and Riya walk into the showroom again. There was a brightness in their steps, the kind of excitement that only comes when love is about to be symbolized forever.

They were back to finalise the center stone.

I smiled and gently called Maya over to the counter. "Come," I said. "Today, I'll show you what *clarity* truly means. Not just the chart... but how I've come to understand it over 40 years of handling thousands of diamonds."

The Thread of the Earth

Each diamond is a frozen flame, formed under the earth by pressure, time, and imperfection. What we call "inclusions" are not flaws in the traditional sense. They are nature's signature, a reminder that beauty doesn't always mean perfection.

To illustrate this, I opened a black velvet case and placed four round diamonds in a row:

1. Flawless (FL)
2. Very Very Slightly Included 1 (VVS1)
3. Very Slightly Included 2 (VS2)
4. Slightly Included 1 (SI1)

Then I handed Maya a loupe and invited her to take a closer look.

Diamond Clarity Comparison

Clarity Grade	**Under 10x Magnification**	**Visibility to Naked Eye**
FL (Flawless)	Completely clean	None
VVS1	Microscopic dot	None
VS2	Tiny crystal off-center	Practically invisible
SI1	Feather on the side	Barely visible (if at all)

As Maya peered through the loupe, she asked, "But why do some diamonds cost so much more when the differences are barely visible?"

I smiled. "That's the paradox of clarity," I said. "Sometimes, what you can't see can cost you dearly and sometimes, what you can see adds more soul than flaw. Let me tell you a story."

I once sold an SI1 diamond to a well-known Bollywood producer. He was known for his perfectionism, so I was surprised when he chose a stone with a visible feather on the side. His words still echo in my mind:

"This inclusion? It's like a scar from a war I won. Let it stay."

Interactive Sidebar: Clarity Isn't Just About Sight

- **Take a hand mirror.** Look closely at yourself. What do you notice that others might never see?
- **Now ask yourself:** Does that make you less valuable or more unique?

Clarity, like self-awareness, isn't always about what others see; it's about what you accept, celebrate, or choose to carry forward. The same applies to diamonds.

How I Judge Clarity

Over the years, clients have asked me how I decide if a diamond is "good enough."

Here's the simple mental checklist I follow:

- Is it **eye-clean**?
- Is the inclusion hidden under a prong?
- Does it affect **brilliance** or **durability**?

If the answer to all three is **no**, then to me and to most of my clients, that diamond is **perfect** for its wearer, no matter what the lab report says.

Riya Asks: "But will it sparkle less?"

I smiled. "My dear, 90% of a diamond's sparkle comes from the cut. Even a flawless diamond can look dull if poorly cut. Clarity is only part of the story."

I paused, letting the weight of that sink in.

- ➢ Flawless diamonds are rare. But beauty? That comes from balance.
- ➢ As a jeweller, I don't just sell diamonds, I match them to people. And like people, the best ones often have a little character inside.

Action Box: Choose Your Ideal Clarity

Here's how I guide clients based on their preferences and priorities:

1. Want a **status symbol or long-term investment**? → Choose **FL** (Flawless) or **IF** (Internally Flawless)
2. Want the **best look with smart value**? → Go for **VS1** or **VS2**
3. Want a **bigger size at a better price**? → Choose **SI1**, but make sure it's *eye-clean* and well-placed!

Why Inclusion Placement Matters More Than the Grade

When purchasing a diamond, many Indian buyers tend to prioritize color and clarity over other factors, believing that a higher clarity grade automatically means a better diamond. This mindset, while common, is only half the truth. While clarity is certainly an important characteristic, it is not the most critical factor in determining a diamond's overall beauty, brilliance, or value.

What Clarity Really Means

Clarity refers to the presence of inclusions (internal flaws like crystals, feathers) and blemishes (surface imperfections) within a diamond. These inclusions are naturally occurring and formed during the diamond's creation process deep within the earth over billions of years.

Clarity is graded on a scale ranging from Flawless (FL) to Included (I1, I2, I3):

- **FL / IF**: No visible inclusions even under magnification
- **VVS / VS**: Very, very slight to very slight inclusions, difficult to detect
- **SI1 / SI2**: Slightly included; inclusions may or may not be visible to the naked eye

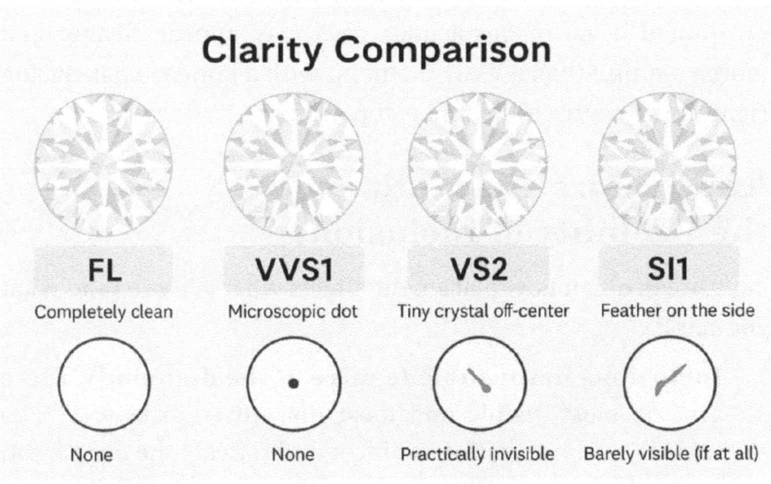

Completely clean (Under 10x Magnification) None

None

Practically invisible

Barely visible (if at all)

However, what truly matters is not just the clarity grade itself, but rather the location, size, and color of the inclusions within the diamond.

Why Inclusion Placement is More Important Than Clarity Grade

To better understand this, consider an analogy:

Imagine two people with birthmarks. One has a larger SI2-sized birthmark, but it is located on their left toe, hidden under their shoe, while the other has a very tiny VVS1-sized birthmark, but it is placed right on their forehead. Even though the second birthmark is much smaller, it is far more noticeable because of its placement.

Similarly, in diamonds, an SI2 clarity diamond with an inclusion positioned in an inconspicuous area may appear cleaner and more beautiful than a VVS1 diamond with a noticeable inclusion right in the centre of its table (top surface).

Key Factors That Influence the Visibility of Inclusions

Let's break down how placement affects what you see (and what you pay):

1. **Inclusions in the table (centre of the diamond)**: These are the most visible and most disruptive to beauty. The table is the largest, flattest facet and reflects the most light, so anything here will be noticed immediately. A visible flaw here can reduce brilliance and even emotional appeal.
2. **Inclusions near the girdle (outer edge of the diamond)**: These are far less visible, especially once the diamond is set in a ring. The prongs or bezel setting can

effectively hide these inclusions, making them practically invisible to the naked eye.

3. **Inclusions under the Crown or Pavilion (angled parts of the diamond):** These may only be visible under magnification and do not impact the diamond's appearance in daily wear.

Thus, an SI1 or SI2 diamond with inclusions near the girdle or hidden beneath the setting can look just as clean and brilliant as a higher-clarity VVS or IF diamond.

The best part? You save significantly on price without compromising on sparkle.

Final Word

Don't judge a diamond only by its certificate.

Judge it by how it makes you feel when it catches the light.

Inclusions tell the story of where a diamond comes from, but your sparkle is defined by where it's going.

LESSON 3

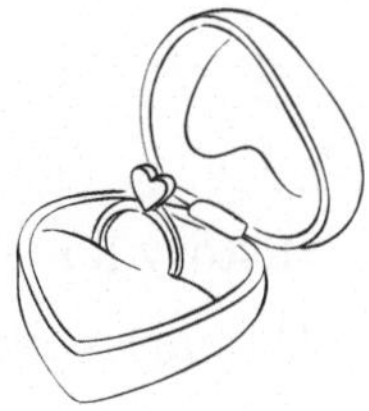

The Ring of Rebirth

Virgin vs. Recycled Gold

DO THEY USE VIRGIN GOLD OR RECYCLED GOLD TO MAKE YOUR DIAMOND ENGAGEMENT RING?

The store had just opened for the day when Mrs. Ritu walked in. She wasn't browsing. She wasn't distracted. She came with purpose, holding a small, faded velvet pouch in one hand and a quiet determination in the other.

"I want to make a new ring," she said, placing the pouch on the counter. But I don't want anything new.

I opened the pouch with care. Inside lay a pair of gold bangles, worn smooth by time, dulled at the edges, but rich in memory. They had stories, perhaps weddings, births, festivals. She had inherited them from her grandmother, now gone.

"This was hers," she said softly. "And I want it to be mine. In a different way."

Gold That Transforms

As a jeweller, I work only with virgin gold straight from the mines, pure, untouched, glowing with youth.

But when I melt **old gold**, I witness something else:

History liquefies.

Memories melt and reform.

Those bangles, once symbols of a grandmother's life, became fluid once again, ready to begin a new journey.

Because **gold never dies**. It only transforms.

But it's not always perfect.

When we recycle gold, **traces of old alloys and impurities** often remain. Some are cleaned. Some stay. It's no longer "pure" in the technical sense, but often, it's richer in sentiment.

The Ethical Choice

I explained the reality to her:

- Most responsible jewellers today prefer recycled gold as it's easier and cheaper than virgin gold.
- Mining for gold often scars the earth, **tons of rock moved for a few grams of metal**.
- Recycled gold skips this damage. It avoids new mining, but the **melting process emits fumes** that can still affect the environment if not handled responsibly.

She listened carefully. Then she smiled: "Then I want this to shine without digging a single new hole in the earth."

And so, we did.

Virgin Gold: Still Noble, Still Desired

Of course, not all clients are the same.

Last week, a groom from Jaipur visited our store. He wanted his engagement ring made with **new 24K virgin gold**, freshly mined from the historic **Kolar mines**.

"It's tradition," he said.

"I want it untouched, just like our beginning."

And that, too, is beautiful.

Because in love, as in life, **your choice matters more than the trend.**

So, What's Your Gold Story?

Is your story one of **renewal**, bringing legacy into the present?

Or one of **tradition**, honoring a new beginning with something untouched?

Would you choose recycled gold to carry your family's memories forward or virgin gold to write a fresh chapter?

There's no right answer. Only the one that feels true to *you*.

What I Made That Day

I crafted her a solitaire ring in 18K yellow gold. At its center sat a modest but brilliant round diamond.

Inside the shank, I engraved the words:

"For all she gave me."

It wasn't just a ring.

It was a conversation between generations, forged in fire, sealed in love.

The Hidden Truth About Recycled Gold

Nothing positive has ever come from using recycled gold, especially since much of it originates from unfortunate events. People typically part with their gold during times of hardship, such as after the loss of a partner or following a divorce. Even more troubling are those who, in moments of desperation, sell their precious jewellery to make ends meet. Additionally, there is a thriving second-hand market and pawn shops that often take advantage of vulnerable sellers.

What's worse, experts suggest that a significant portion of gold circulating in the second-hand market may be stolen, melted down and passed off as "clean" recycled gold to avoid detection. In most cases, this gold carries a history of misfortune and negativity. Many people believe that jewellery made from recycled gold carries bad karma, which is then transferred to the new owner, bringing misfortune to their relationship or celebration.

For this reason, we do not use recycled gold in our diamond engagement rings and jewellery. We want our customers to begin their new journeys with something pure, free from the burdens of past misfortunes.

Engagements and weddings are joyous occasions, celebrating new beginnings. They should be marked with the purity of new gold, ensuring that these special moments are not tainted by any lingering negativity. After all, an engagement or wedding is a once-in-a-lifetime event and it deserves to be celebrated with the finest.

Furthermore, recycled gold often contains impurities that can affect the quality and durability of the final piece. One such issue is porosity, which can make a ring brittle and prone to breaking. When recycled gold is not properly refined, it may introduce microscopic flaws that weakens the metal over time.

This is yet another reason why we choose to use only fresh, virgin gold, so your jewellery remains strong, beautiful, and enduring.

LESSON 4

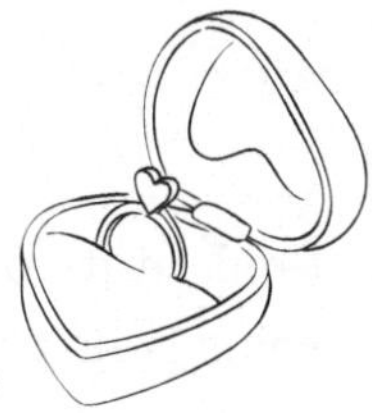

Beyond Yellow

The Hidden Science of Gold's Colors

WHAT PROCESS DO THEY FOLLOW TO TURN YELLOW GOLD INTO WHITE OR PINK GOLD?

White Gold Comparison: Plated vs. Solid

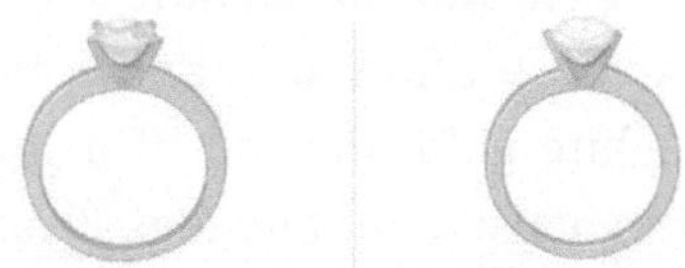

Rhodium-Plated White Gold	Solid White Gold (Palladium Alloy)
Color Source Surface may wear off over time	**Naturally white** from within
Maintenance Needs re-plating every 1-2 years	**Color and strength** remain lifelong
Cost Lower initial cost	**Higher initial cost,** lower long-term maintenance
Can fade, exposing yellow gold underneath	**Stays white and bright** permanently
Feel & Weight Slightly lighter	**Heavier, with a more luxurious feel**

Gold, in its purest form, has a naturally rich yellow color. This color is its true identity, born from its unique atomic structure and chemical makeup. But the gold you see in modern jewellery isn't always yellow. To create white or pink gold, jewellers must engage in a carefully controlled process of alloying, mixing gold with other metals to change both its color and its properties.

From Yellow to White: The Making of White Gold

To achieve white gold, palladium, a rare and precious metal from the platinum family, is typically added to pure gold. This method is both costly and complex. Palladium not only commands a high market price but also requires precision to blend it correctly, ensuring the final product maintains its brilliance, strength, and a uniform white appearance.

Because of the high cost and the technical skill involved, many jewellers opt for a more affordable and less labour-intensive method to create white gold. Instead of using palladium, they mix gold with less expensive metals like silver and nickel. This creates a base metal that has a lighter color, which is then coated with a thin layer of rhodium. Rhodium is a silvery-white metal that belongs to the platinum group and is often used in jewellery for its reflective finish and resistance to tarnishing.

The process of rhodium plating involves electroplating, where a thin layer of rhodium is applied to the surface of yellow gold. This gives the gold a white appearance and helps to increase its resistance to corrosion, making the piece look shinier and more durable. However, there are a few important points to note about rhodium plating:

a. **Temporary Nature of Plating:** The rhodium coating is not permanent and can wear off over time, especially with regular wear. This is because the thin layer of rhodium is vulnerable to scratching and fading, which means the gold underneath may start to show through after a while.

b. **Adhesion Issues:** The plating process can sometimes fail to adhere properly to the gold if the yellow gold contains certain alloys. In such cases, the rhodium layer may not bond well, leading to uneven or peeling plating.

c. **Ongoing Maintenance:** Once the rhodium plating begins to fade, it can be re-applied, but this requires an additional cost and effort.

A Better Option: Solid White Gold

An alternative to rhodium plating for achieving white gold is a more permanent method: creating a mold of the piece and casting it directly in white gold. This process involves mixing gold with palladium and sometimes other metals to form an alloy that is naturally white in color. The resulting piece is more durable and its color is consistent throughout, unlike rhodium-plated gold, where the coating can wear off and reveal the yellow gold beneath.

This method offers a key advantage: the **color is permanent**. Unlike rhodium-plated gold, where the white finish wears off over time to reveal the yellow base beneath, solid white gold retains its hue throughout the piece, through every polish, scratch, and celebration.

Additionally, because the gold is alloyed with palladium, it gains the strength and corrosion resistance of the platinum family. This means the piece is not only more beautiful but also more resilient, making it ideal for daily wear, heirloom designs, or once-in-a-lifetime jewellery like engagement rings and wedding bands.

White Gold Comparison: Plated vs. Solid

Feature	Rhodium-Plated White Gold	Solid White Gold (Palladium Alloy)
Color Source	Coated with rhodium to look white	Naturally white from within
Durability	Surface may wear off over time	Color and strength remain lifelong
Maintenance	Needs re-plating every 1–2 years	No re-plating required
Cost	Lower initial cost	Higher initial cost, lower long-term maintenance
Look Over Time	Can fade, exposing yellow gold underneath	Stays white and bright permanently
Feel & Weight	Slightly lighter	Heavier, with a more luxurious feel
Ideal For	Temporary or budget-friendly options	Heirlooms, wedding rings, lasting luxury

In summary, while rhodium-plated gold can offer an affordable way to achieve a white or silvery appearance, it does come with the drawback of needing maintenance over time. For those seeking a more lasting **low-maintenance**, and truly luxurious solution, solid white gold crafted with palladium is undoubtedly the better choice, offering enduring color, superior strength, and timeless elegance.

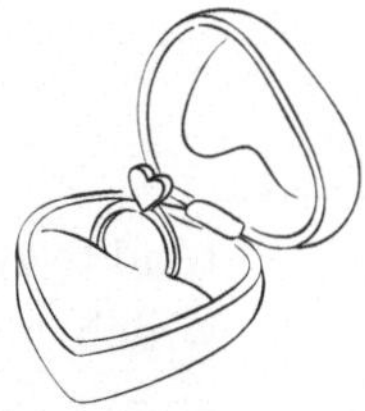

LESSON 5

Comfort Fit vs. Regular Fit
The Inside Story of Your Ring

DID THEY EXPLAIN THE DIFFERENCE BETWEEN COMFORT-FIT AND REGULAR-FIT OR JUST SKIPPED IT?

When it comes to wearing a ring every day, especially something as personal as a wedding band, comfort is not a luxury, it's a necessity.

A comfort-fit ring is specially designed with a domed interior, meaning the inside surface of the ring is slightly rounded rather than flat. This subtle curve makes a significant difference: it allows the ring to make less direct contact with the skin, offering a more ergonomic and comfortable fit.

On the other hand, standard-fit rings have a flat inner surface, which can feel tighter and more restrictive over time.

Advantages of a Comfort-Fit Ring

1. **Easier to Slide Over the Knuckle**

   One of the most noticeable benefits of a comfort-fit ring is how effortlessly it glides over the knuckle. The domed interior reduces resistance, making it especially beneficial for individuals with larger knuckles or those whose fingers tend to swell throughout the day. Unlike standard-fit rings, which can feel tight or difficult to remove, comfort-fit rings ensure a smoother transition over the knuckle, making them easier to wear and remove at any time.

2. **Reduced Friction and Enhanced Wear ability**

   The rounded interior reduces friction between the metal and the skin, minimizing irritation and discomfort. This makes comfort-fit rings ideal for daily wear, especially for wedding bands meant to be worn continuously. The gentle contouring of the inner band distributes pressure more evenly across the finger, reducing the risk of pinching, chafing, or soreness, issues that are more common with flat, standard-fit designs.

3. **Increased Durability and Luxury Feel**

   Comfort-fit rings are often crafted using more metal than standard-fit rings, giving them a slightly thicker profile. This added thickness enhances durability and provides a more substantial, luxurious feel. While they may be slightly heavier, the superior comfort they offer makes them a preferred choice for many wearers.

Challenges in Making a Comfort-Fit Diamond Ring

While comfort-fit rings offer superior comfort and durability, they come with production challenges, especially when diamonds are involved.

- First, the additional metal used naturally increases **material costs**.
- Second, the **domed interior** requires more **time, tools, and skill** to shape correctly.

Setting diamonds into such a ring is no easy task. The rounded interior means jewellers must carefully adjust the setting process to ensure that diamonds are securely placed without affecting the ring's ergonomic design. This additional complexity requires more time and precision, driving up production costs. Because of these challenges, many jewellers avoid making diamond rings with a comfort-fit design, instead opting for the simpler and more cost-effective standard fit. However, for those who prioritize long-term comfort and quality, the extra investment in a comfort-fit diamond ring is well worth it.

Conclusion: Designed for a Lifetime

A comfort-fit ring offers exceptional ease of wear, making it a popular choice for individuals who wear their rings daily. Its unique domed interior reduces friction, allows for a smoother fit, and enhances durability.

Yes, it may require more metal and more craftsmanship which makes it pricier but this extra investment pays off in the long run.

For those who believe a ring should feel as good as it looks, especially one that marks a milestone like an engagement or wedding, the comfort-fit ring is more than a choice, it's a commitment to lasting comfort and elegance.

LESSON 6

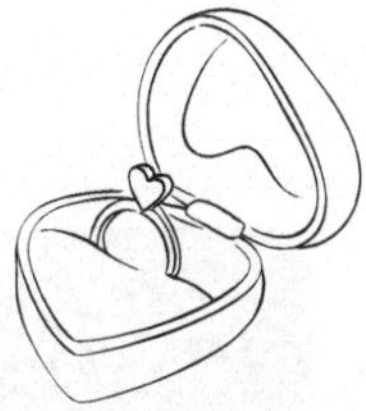

Beyond the Cut Grade
The Hidden Keys to Unrivaled Sparkle

WHY DO SOME DIAMONDS SPARKLE MORE THAN OTHERS DESPITE HAVING AN EXCELLENT CUT?

Even if two diamonds share the same excellent cut grade, their sparkle can still differ. One of the lesser-known reasons behind this variation is fluorescence.

Fluorescence is the way a diamond reacts to ultraviolet (UV) light. Some diamonds emit a soft glow, usually blue, when exposed to UV rays, such as sunlight or certain artificial lights. This phenomenon, though often overlooked, can subtly influence a diamond's overall appearance, either enhancing or diminishing its brilliance, depending on the context.

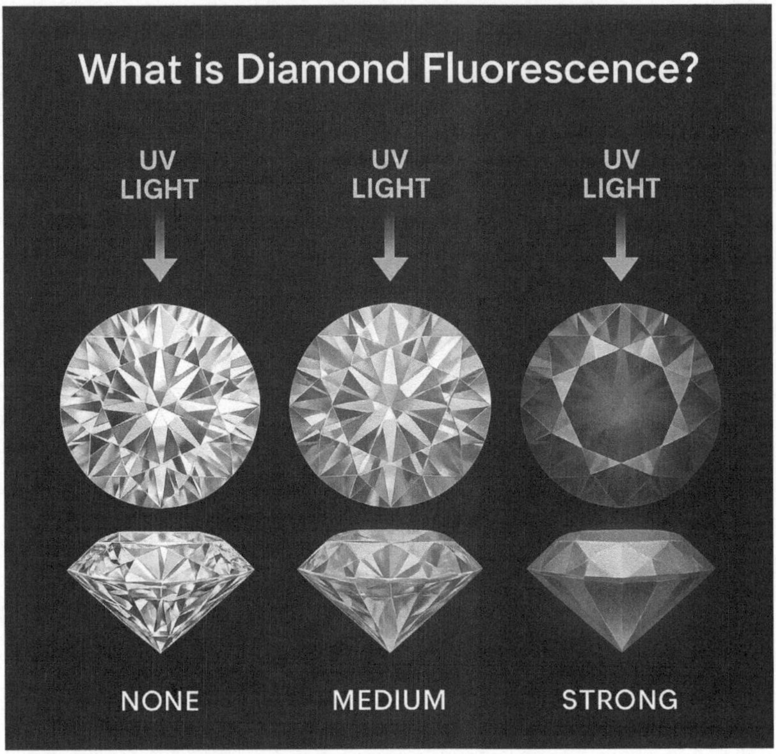

Here's how fluorescence affects a diamond's sparkle:

1. **Strong Fluorescence Can Create a Hazy Look**: Diamonds with very strong fluorescence may sometimes appear cloudy or milky, especially under natural light. This haziness reduces the diamond's ability to reflect light efficiently, making it look less vibrant or dull, even if it has been cut to perfection. A high-quality cut can't always compensate for this internal cloudiness caused by overactive fluorescence.
2. **Fluorescence Can Improve Color in Lower-Grade Diamonds**: In diamonds with a slight yellow tint (e.g., grades J, K, or lower), blue fluorescence can work to your advantage.

It can visually counteract the yellowish tones, making the diamond appear whiter and brighter than its grade suggests. For buyers looking for a balance between beauty and budget, such diamonds can be a smart choice, if the fluorescence is moderate and well-matched to the diamond's color.

3. **Minimal or Faint Fluorescence Has Little to No Effect** – Most diamonds with faint to medium fluorescence do not show any noticeable difference in sparkle under normal lighting conditions. Their brilliance and fire remain intact, and any glow under UV light is typically subtle, making these diamonds safe choices for those concerned about appearance.
4. **Impact in Different Lighting Conditions** – Fluorescence tends to reveal itself under strong UV light, such as direct sunlight or club lighting, where the diamond may emit a visible glow. In everyday indoor lighting, however, this effect is usually negligible or entirely unnoticeable. Still, if you're buying a diamond for frequent wear in varied environments, it's wise to see how it behaves in both natural and artificial light before making a decision.

Conclusion

While fluorescence does not always negatively impact a diamond's brilliance, strong fluorescence in certain diamonds can slightly reduce clarity and affect how much light is reflected, making them appear less sparkly than others with the same excellent cut.

LESSON 7

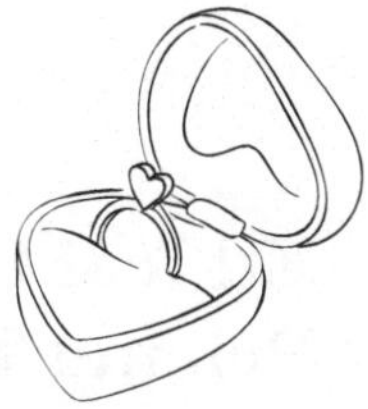

Beyond the "D"
What Your Diamond's Color & Conscience Really Mean

HOW DOES DIAMOND COLOR CONNECT TO ETHICS AND PRICING?

Diamonds from various sources, including South Africa, Canada, and Russia, often exhibit a subtle yellow or brown tint. In the diamond trade, these stones are commonly referred to as **"Syndicate Diamonds."** Among them, diamonds with a brownish hue tend to be valued lower than those with a yellow tint, even if their clarity and cut are similar.

A peculiar and noteworthy characteristic of **Zimbabwean diamonds** is their greenish tint. In fact, **more than 50% of the world's green diamonds** originate from Zimbabwe, and it is widely believed that almost all green-tinted diamonds found in the Indian market come from this region. These diamonds can range in tone, from a **very light green hue** to a **darker, yellowish-green** and can sometimes appear **murky or dull**, which affects their perceived value.

Ethical Considerations and Pricing Transparency

When purchasing a diamond, it is crucial to ensure that it comes from a legitimate and ethical source. Syndicate Diamonds, sourced through legally recognized channels, are the only diamonds buyers should consider. These diamonds are traded transparently and adhere to international ethical standards, providing peace of mind to the buyer.

Unfortunately, some jewellers fail to disclose the true origin of their diamonds, leading buyers to unknowingly purchase stones from questionable or unethical sources. Zimbabwean diamonds, for instance, generally trade at lower prices due to their greenish tint. However, if a jeweller does not disclose this, customers may end up paying the same price for a Zimbabwean diamond as they would for a higher-value, yellow-tinted Syndicate Diamond.

Avoiding Blood Diamonds

Beyond color and pricing, the most important factor when purchasing a diamond is its ethical origin. Conflict diamonds, commonly referred to as **blood diamonds**, are mined in war zones and sold to finance armed conflicts and human rights abuses. Many of these diamonds have historically come from politically unstable regions, including parts of Africa.

While international sanctions on Zimbabwean diamonds have been lifted, it remains the buyer's responsibility to ensure that their diamond is sourced legally and ethically. The **Kimberley Process Certification Scheme (KPCS)** was established to prevent the trade of blood diamonds, but loopholes still exist. This makes it essential for buyers to request proper certification and documentation from reputable jewellers.

This is why it is essential, now more than ever, for buyers to ask for proper documentation and certification from reputable jewellers. A certificate not only verifies the diamond's quality but also confirms that your purchase doesn't contribute to conflict, exploitation, or unethical trade practices.

Making an Informed Purchase

To protect yourself from overpaying and to ensure ethical sourcing, follow these guidelines when purchasing a diamond:

1. **Insist on Syndicate Diamonds**: Choose diamonds that originate from recognized, legal sources such as South Africa, Canada, and Russia.
2. **Verify Certification**: Always request proper certification. Look for a **Kimberley Process Certificate** or documentation from reputable gemological institutions like **GIA (Gemological Institute of America)** or **IGI (International Gemological Institute)**. These ensure both quality and ethical sourcing.
3. **Be Cautious of Green-Tinted Diamonds**: If a diamond has a greenish hue, confirm its origin and ensure that its price reflects its true market value.
4. **Buy from Trusted Jewellers**: Purchase only from well-established, ethical jewellers who disclose full details about a diamond's origin.

By taking these precautions, buyers can ensure they are investing in a legally sourced, high-quality diamond while also promoting ethical practices in the global diamond trade.

LESSON 8

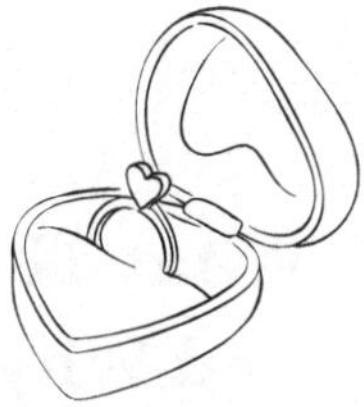

The Hidden Fixes
Diamond Enhancements Your Jeweller Explains (or Hides)

Understanding Diamond Enhancement Terms: What Do They Mean?

When shopping for a diamond, you may come across terms like *laser enhanced, laser path, heat treated,* or *fracture filled*. These are not words you want to hear from a reputable jeweller. If a jeweller mentions any of these terms or if they appear in a diamond's description, it's often a red flag that the diamond has undergone artificial treatments to improve its appearance.

While these treatments may make a diamond look more appealing at first glance, they can significantly impact the stone's value, durability, and long-term beauty. It's important to know exactly what you're paying for and what's been done to the stone.

What These Terms Mean and Why They Matter?

1. **Laser Enhanced / Laser Path Diamonds**
    - This technique is used to remove dark inclusions (flaws) within a diamond by burning tiny pathways (laser paths) to the inclusion and then bleaching it with acid.
    - While this makes the diamond appear cleaner, those laser-drilled channels remain permanently within the stone, weakening its structure.
    - As a result, a laser-enhanced diamond is worth much less than a natural, untreated diamond with the same clarity.
2. **Fracture-Filled Diamonds**
    - A process where a glass-like substance is injected into cracks (fractures) within a diamond to make them less visible.
    - Over time, this filling can degrade, turning cloudy or even falling out, revealing the original cracks.
    - Fracture-filled diamonds are much weaker than untreated diamonds and can break apart unexpectedly.
    - They are also highly sensitive to heat, pressure, and even everyday wear.
3. **Heat-Treated Diamonds**
    - This process involves heating a diamond at high temperatures to improve or change its color.
    - Some heat treatments are stable, but others can fade or discolor over time, especially when exposed to strong light or chemicals.

- Heat treatment can also weaken the diamond's crystal structure, making it more fragile and less durable.

Why Do These Treatments Hurt the Diamond's Value and Longevity?

While these treatments may make a diamond look flawless temporarily, they often create long-term issues. Many of these techniques are simply short-term fixes used by less reputable dealers to sell lower-quality diamonds at higher prices. The biggest risks include:

- **Reduced Value:** Enhanced diamonds typically have far lower resale value compared to untreated stones of the same clarity and color.
- **Durability Issues:** Some enhancements weaken the diamond, making it more prone to chipping, cracking, or breaking unexpectedly.
- **Unstable Appearance:** Fracture filling and some heat treatments can degrade over time, leading to noticeable changes in the diamond's clarity and color.

Know Your Rights: Full Disclosure is Required

By law, **full disclosure is mandatory** when a diamond has undergone any type of enhancement. Jewellers are required to inform buyers of such treatments, and this information should also appear on the diamond's official certification.

Always request a certificate from a **trusted authority**, such as **GIA, IGI, or AGS** and **carefully read** the report for any mention of enhancements.

If a jeweller is vague, avoids the subject, or refuses to provide documentation, it's a major warning sign. Walk away.

Bottom Line

A high-quality and untreated diamond is more than just a purchase; it's a lasting investment in value, beauty, and peace of mind. Enhanced diamonds might seem attractive upfront, but they often cannot guarantee long-term performance or retained worth. Always choose clarity, in both the stone and the seller.

LESSON 9

What Are the Benefits of Purchasing an Engagement Ring from Us?

Our Answer: We are VERY different from other stores. It is quite rare to have the opportunity to work directly with the artist who will be creating your ring. But with us, that's exactly what happens. There's zero room for miscommunication because nothing goes through a "salesperson." You **work-one-on-one with the designer** of your ring throughout the entire creation process, from the very first idea to the final polish.

We put a tremendous amount of time and energy into creating each ring and this is why **we have a perfect 100% rating of happy clients** (we've literally never had a client dislike their ring... EVER).

The 'Making of Your Ring' Video: A World-First Experience

We also offer something completely unique: the **'Making of Your Ring'** video service, the only one of its kind in the world (yes, we've checked!)

Here's how it works

This video captures the entire process of creating your partner's engagement ring. We even include a short interview with you, where you share heartfelt thoughts about your partner. That voiceover is then layered onto footage of the ring being handcrafted, making it a truly personal and emotional keepsake.

Partners absolutely LOVE it. Our whole purpose as a jeweller is to make the moment where you present the engagement ring the most amazing memory ever. Based on how people react to the film, it really makes each piece a cherished work of art. This film will make you look VERY romantic.

It's not a requirement to do the film as a client of Gandaram jewellers, but it's a special service we offer if you're interested.

Conclusion

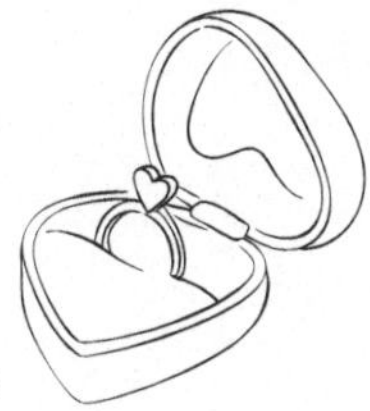

Choose Smartly, Wear Proudly

Your engagement ring is more than just a piece of jewellery; it's a timeless symbol of love, commitment, and a promise that lasts a lifetime. When making such an important purchase, you deserve nothing less than exceptional quality, transparency, and expert craftsmanship.

At Gandaram Jewellers, we are committed to providing only the finest, ethically sourced, and meticulously crafted diamonds, ensuring that your ring not only looks stunning today but remains a cherished heirloom for generations. Unlike other jewellers who may cut corners with treated or lower-quality stones, we guarantee 100% natural, high-quality diamonds that sparkle with unmatched brilliance. Because we believe that your love story deserves nothing but the very best.

This is your love story, your once-in-a-lifetime moment, make it extraordinary with a diamond ring that truly reflects its significance. Choose quality. Choose trust. Choose Gandaram Jewellers.

Connect With Us

Visit: www.gandaramjewellers.com

Or scan the QR code to connect with us via WhatsApp

Call: +919810060352

Email: puneet@gandaramjewellers.com,

info@gandaramjewellers.com, grjewels@hotmail.com

Showroom Locations:

Noida Store

(https://share.google/BSKHcTiDzi6w87YD0)

Lajpat Nagar Store

(https://g.co/kgs/DrLe7H)